The Appalachian Trail

An Aerial View

Mark Warner

THE APPALACHIAN TRAIL: AN AERIAL VIEW

Copyright © 2004 by Mark Warner

This book is not intended to be a guidebook of any sort to the Appalachian Trail, but rather an aerial survey of some of the more scenic and popular locations on the trail. Any errors in position or placement are the author's.
Except where noted, all photographs are by the author.

Jacket photographs:

    Front: Franconia Ridge, NH
    Back (top): View looking northeast at Mount Washington and the White Mountains, NH
    Back (bottom): Chestnut Knob, VA

    Title page photographs:

    Center: View looking northeast at Mount Washington and the White Mountains, NH
    Lower left: Chestnut Knob, VA
    Lower right: Mount Avery, NH

    Dedication (pg 9) photograph:

    View over Georgia mountains

Edited and designed by Michael Steere
Maps by Olive Metcalf

ISBN 0-9661382-2-8

Printed in China by Jade Productions

    5   4   3   2   1

1. Appalachian Trail – Description and travel. 2. Aerial views – Appalachian Trail.
3. Aviation – flying the Appalachian Trail. 4. Appalachian Trail – aerial views.

Library of Congress Control Number: 2004106549

Acknowledgments

I would like to thank the following people and organizations for their valuable assistance and information:

The Appalachian Trail Conference, Harpers Ferry, West Virginia, for their trail guides and trail maps; the Maine Appalachian Trail Club for their *Appalachian Trail Guide to Maine;* the Keystone Trails Association for their *Appalachian Trail Guide to Pennsylvania*; DeLorme in Yarmouth, Maine for their wonderful Atlases and Gazetteers; Jim Chase and his *Guide to the Appalachian Trail;* Stackpole Books for their *Exploring the Appalachian Trail* series; V. Collins Chew and his *Under Foot, A Geologic Guide to the Appalachian Trail*; David Edwin Lillard for his *Appalachian Trail Names;* Larry Luxenberg for *Walking the Appalachian Trail;* Victoria and Frank Logue for their *Best of the Appalachian Day Hikes;* and last, but certainly not least, Bill Bryson for his *A Walk in the Woods*.

Also, Mark "The Biker Sly" Nienstaedt for being at Springer and wearing a bright yellow shirt; George "Statesman" Hebard for first enlightening me about the AT and planting the seed for the book; Mike Muchmore and Ann Walko of Wicked Good Aviation, Wiscasset, Maine for keeping the Cubs flying; Jim Tatum of Habersham Aviation, Habersham County Airport, Cornelia, Georgia; Ben Rider of Rider Jet Center, Hagerstown Regional Airport, Hagerstown, Maryland; Dr. M. A. "Trip" Bowers, David Glass, Reini Schmidt and Brian Pruett of Elizabethton Minicipal Airport, Elizabethton, Tennessee for getting me over the AT when I couldn't get the Cub out of Maine due to bad weather. Thanks also to Kathy and Helen for the E-mails, Lucy Kuemmerle for the proofreading and special thanks to Michael Steere for his editing and great design work. Thanks also to those unidentified individuals I met along the trail for their input.

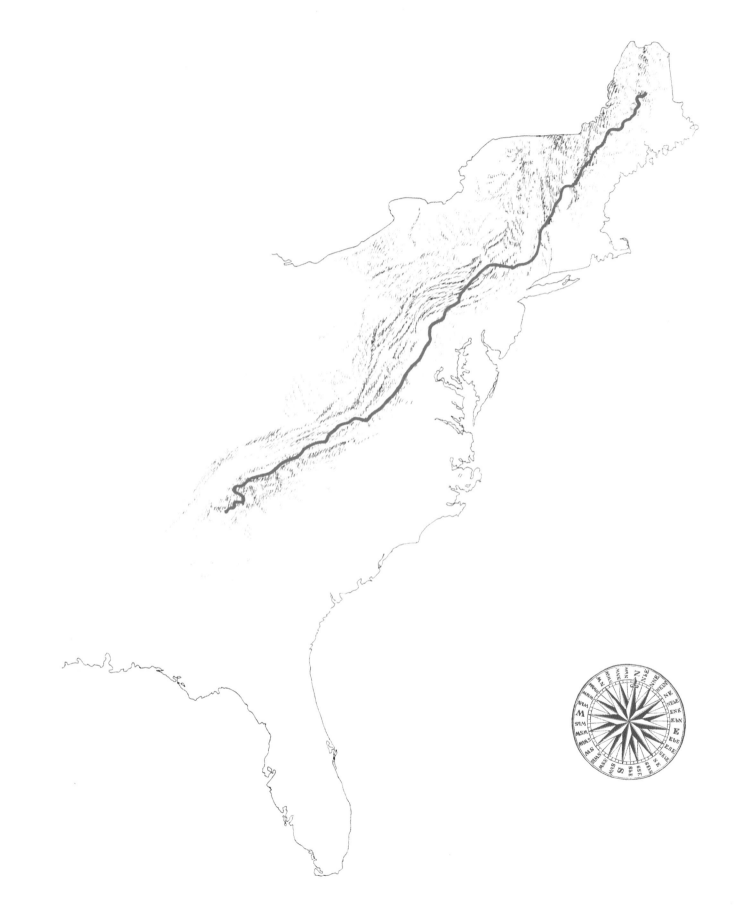

Contents

C
O
N
T
E
N
T
S

Appalachian Trail thru-hiker signing in on Springer Mountain, Georgia

Introduction

The Appalachian Trail was the longest, continuous trail in the world until 1993, when the Pacific Crest Trail was completed. The AT may no longer be the longest, but it is perhaps the most popular. A little over two thousand miles in length, it follows the ridges of the Appalachian Mountains from Georgia to Maine. It is estimated that approximately four million people use the AT each year. Some are day hikers, while others hike only on weekends or for a week or more. There are section hikers, who hike long stretches at a time—for example, a whole state's portion of the trail. The minority, and perhaps the most elite, are the thru-hikers, who do the entire trail in one year.

In 1921, there were a number of hiking trails in the eastern United States, but most were short in length. This situation changed when Benton MacKaye, a research forester with the U.S. Forest Service, published an article in the *Journal of the American Institute of Architects* entitled, "An Appalachian Trail, a Project in Regional Planning." His vision was a long trail running from New Hampshire's Mount Washington to Mount Mitchell in North Carolina. The first section of trail to be completed was forty miles in New York's Bear Mountain State Park. It may have been Benton MacKaye's concept, but it took Myron Avery of Maine and Judge Arthur Perkins of Connecticut to provide the organizational skills and drive to put it all together. Maine's Mount Katahdin won out over Mount Washington as the northern terminus, and the southern end was moved further south to Mount Oglethorpe in Georgia. The Appalachian Trail was completed in 1937, but much work remained to ensure its protection.

The National Trail Systems Act became law in 1968 and was further amended by the Appalachian Trail Amendment. As of 2004, over 99.4 percent of the AT is now fully protected in national parks, national forests, state forests, state parks and on private lands. The official overseer of the AT is the National Park Service, but the actual running of the trail is left to the Appalachian Trail Conference, headquartered in Harpers Ferry, West Virginia. Thirty-one hiking clubs are responsible for maintaining the trail; the actual work is done by thousands of volunteers who spend countless hours trimming, clearing, fortifying sections of the trail, moving parts of it as needed, building steps at difficult areas, making repairs to over two hundred shelters and many other tasks.

The Appalachian Mountains themselves begin in Alabama, run roughly northeast to Maine, continue on into eastern Canada, across Newfoundland, duck under the Atlantic Ocean and re-emerge in Scotland and Norway, where they end. All told, the range is over four thousand miles in length. The Appalachians are hundreds of millions of years old—the oldest mountains in North America. What we see today is the result of erosion that has been wearing the mountains down for the past forty million years or so since the last bit of uplifting. The last ice age covered the northern section of the Appalachians down to Pennsylvania and retreated about ten thousand years ago, leaving much evidence of its presence.

As of 2004, the official length of the Appalachian Trail is 2,174.16 miles. This figure, however, is by no means final, as the trail is continually shifted here and there to avoid encroaching development and bad sections, and to provide hikers with better views. The trail starts in northwest Georgia and goes through thirteen more states, in order, North Carolina, Tennessee, Virginia, West Virginia, Maryland, Pennsylvania, New Jersey, New York, Connecticut, Massachusetts, Vermont, New Hampshire and, finally, Maine. The longest section within a single state is the more than 500 miles that pass through Virginia—a quarter of the entire AT. The shortest state section is in West Virginia, at less than twenty miles. The highest mountain is Clingmans Dome on the North Carolina-Tennessee border at 6,643 feet in elevation. The lowest part of the trail is at Bear Mountain State Park, in New York, at 124 feet above sea level. The Appalachian Trail is very diverse; it runs over ridges, mountain peaks, down through gaps and notches, across meadows and fields, crosses rivers on bridges and even runs through towns. Join us on a visual tour of the trail by air, from Georgia to Maine. The perspective from a small airplane is unique!

Each chapter begins with a small ground photograph of a particular spot on the trail for that state. See if you can identify them. They'll be identified on the following page, lower left corner. This location is the trail up Warner Hill in Massachusetts; the ferns provide a clue.

8

Afoot and light-hearted, I take to the open road,
healthy, free, the world before me.

— Walt Whitman, "Song of the Open Road"

This book is dedicated to the thousands of AT volunteers from Georgie to Maine.

Without them there would be no trail.

And to Helen for too many reasons.

Without her, there would be no book.

Approach trail to Springer Mountain at Amicalola State Park, Georgia

Georgia

"Georgia is hard," the woman said, resting on the side of the trail at Woody Gap. She should know, as she had hiked the entire trail from Georgia to Maine several years earlier. Now she was doing it again, but with her two sons this time. Some consider Georgia one of the most difficult of the fourteen states the Appalachian Trail passes through. This is due in part to the ruggedness of the terrain, but also to the fact that people don't think of Georgia as being that tough. After all, most of the state is quite flat. I encountered two gentlemen just north of Springer Mountain, the southern end of the AT, who were already quitting their thru-hike to Maine. When asked why, one of them replied, "We had no idea this was going to be so difficult."

Seen in profile, the Appalachian mountains of Georgia resemble the teeth of a saw—mountain peak, a valley called a gap, another mountain, another gap and so on. There are five major gaps on the AT in Georgia and some thirty smaller ones. The trail is oriented northeast-southwest along the eastern ridge of the Blue Ridge Mountains and runs for a little over seventy-five miles to the North Carolina border.

Glaciers never reached this far south, and the Appalachians have suffered millions of years of weathering and erosion in the warm climate. The trail, running along the ridges and through the gaps, is mostly clay mixed with humus. There is a great deal of mica present, which makes the trail sparkle in the sunlight. Many thru-hikers, beginning their journey in mid-March or even April, encounter snow, which adds to the difficulty of the trail in Georgia.

The Appalachian Trail originally began on Mount Oglethorpe, some twenty miles to the southeast of Springer. Encroaching development threatened the Oglethorpe site, and it was moved in 1958. The entire length of the Appalachian Trail in Georgia is now fully protected, as it lies completely within the borders of the Chattahoochee National Forest. Georgia thus became one of the very first states to have its portion of the Appalachian Trail totally protected.

G E O R G I A

Mount Oglethorpe, named for one of Georgia's founders, was the original southern end of the Appalachian Trail. Encroaching development, plus the trail's course through many private lands, caused a change to the beginning of the trail in 1958. The southern beginning of the AT was thus moved thirteen miles (as the crow flies) northeast to Springer Mountain and the protection of the Chattahoochee National Forest.

Preceding page: Springer Mountain

For many, Amicalola State Park, in northwestern Georgia, is the beginning of the Appalachian Trail experience. Like many of the geographical features of the area, the name comes from the Cherokee "ama" (meaning water) and "kalola" (tumbling). The tumbling water at Amicalola, a little over 700 feet in height, is the highest waterfall east of the Mississippi River.

Springer Mountain, the present southern terminus of the Appalachian Trail, lies at 3,782 feet in elevation. Once called Penitentiary Mountain, Springer is believed to be named for the first Presbyterian minister of Georgia. The gently rounded and wooded mountain is an unassuming beginning for a trail that stretches more than two thousand miles to Maine.

The fire tower on Black Mountain looks down on Woody Gap to the right. The tower has not been manned for many years and is no longer used for fire-spotting. The Appalachian Trail runs past below and just to the right. Although the building is closed to the public due to its poor condition, many hikers make the short side trip up for the fine views from Black Mountain.

Woody Gap is one of five major gaps that cut across the Appalachian Trail in Georgia. Woody Gap is twenty miles north of Springer Mountain and the first highway that a northbound hiker would come to. For supplies, the town of Suches is only a couple of miles down the road (to the left in the picture).

The highest elevation of the AT in Georgia is on Blood Mountain, at 4461 feet. This is a popular day hike, as it is only 2.4 miles from Neels Gap. The strenuous trip rewards the hiker with spectacular views from the rocky summit. Blood Mountain is named for a battle between the Cherokee and the Creeks which was so fierce that their blood supposedly stained the rocks red. It may also be that certain lichens on the summit take on a reddish color when wet.

The two room shelter on Blood Mountain was built in the '30s by the Civilian Conservation Corps. This mountain is one of the most popular day hikes on the entire AT, and on weekends the summit can get quite crowded.

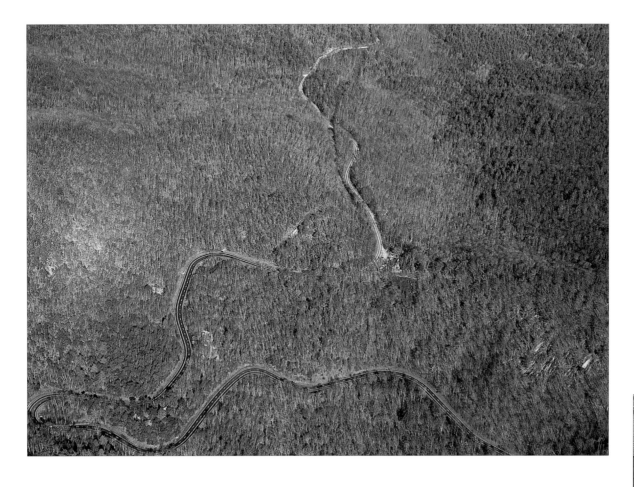

Neels Gap is immediately east of Blood Mountain. The complex of buildings on the road curve is Mountain Crossings at Walasi-Yi. Here hikers can get groceries, take a shower, do laundry, spend the night or make a telephone call. Mountain Crossings also has a store specializing in outdoor equipment. The breezeway between the store and the living quarters is the only place where the AT passes through a building.

Wolf Laurel Top Mountain, at 3,766 feet in elevation, offers excellent views to the south toward the Raven Cliffs Wilderness Area.

Some of the best views in Georgia are from Tray Mountain in the Tray Mountain Wilderness Area. The name is believed to come from an Indian word meaning "trail," as there are many of them leading to the summit of Tray Mountain. The U.S. Forest Service built the Tray Mountain shelter in 1971. At 4,430 feet, Tray Mountain is one of Georgia's finest peaks.

Lookout Mountain Scenic Highway U.S. 76 cuts through Dicks Creek Gap. A small parking lot and picnic table are located here. Dicks Creek Gap is only 8.8 miles south of the North Carolina border.

North Carolina & Tennessee

Since most of the AT in these states runs along the border between North Carolina and Tennessee, the two are covered together in this one chapter. The total distance of the trail in these two states is about 350 miles, with much of it above 5,000 feet. The AT goes through three national forests: Nantahala, Pisgah, and Cherokee. It also includes the Great Smoky Mountains National Park, two large dams and some of the oldest rocks in the world. Clingmans Dome, on the western edge of the national park, is the highest peak of the entire AT at 6,643 feet above sea level.

The Appalachian Trail in North Carolina runs north for approximately ninety miles from the Georgia border to Fontana Dam. Many hikers consider this section of the trail through the Nantahalas to be one of the most rugged on the whole AT, except for New Hampshire and Maine. From the dam, it then goes about five miles north to the Tennessee border. From there, the trail follows the North Carolina-Tennessee border all the way to Virginia, except for a 40-mile Tennessee stretch in the vicinity of Watauga Lake and Iron Mountain.

The trail itself is mostly ridge hiking with many sections above five thousand feet. The lowest point of the AT in these two states is the Nantahala River at Wesser, North Carolina. This middle part of the trail, especially on the North Carolina-Tennessee border, goes over the wonderful southern balds—open, grassy mountain tops.

Albert Mountain, at 5,250 feet, is nearly a mile high. Like many other mountains in North Carolina and Tennessee, an elevation over five thousand feet is not uncommon. The fire tower is no longer manned, but is accessible to hikers who want to gain a better view.

Preceding page: Carvers Gap, North Carolina

Located in the Nantahala Mountains, Wayah Bald sits at 5,432 feet. The stone observation tower was built in 1935 by the Civilian Conservation Corps, and offers fine views toward the Smoky Mountains and into the valley below. As you can see, the mountain top is no longer bald.

The Tennessee Valley Authority constructed Fontana Dam from 1942–'45. At 480 feet, it is the highest dam in the eastern United States. The trail goes across the top of the dam and provides a great view down Fontana Lake. The lake, created by the blocked Little Tennessee River, forms the southern boundary of the Great Smoky National Park. The dam was built to supply electricity to Alcoa, for the production of aluminum, and to the labratory at Oak Ridge, for its work on the Manhattan Project. Two miles west of the dam is Fontana Village, which offers lodging, food, laundry and other services for hikers.

26

Clingmans Dome, at 6,643 feet, is the highest point on the entire Appalachian Trail. It also offers the longest stretch of AT ridge trail above five thousand feet. Easy access via an automobile road makes Clingmans a popular destination. The observation tower provides outstanding views in all directions. Clingmans Dome was originally called Smoky Dome, but was renamed for Thomas L. Clingman, a Civil War general and United States senator. Situated right on the border between North Carolina and Tennessee, Clingmans Dome is located on the northern boundary of the Great Smoky National Park.

The rocky knob to the left of the prominent peak is Charlies Bunion. Formed from cracked slate, the footing can be dangerous in wet weather. Hikers have been injured here, and some have fallen to their death. Charlies Bunion is named in honor of Charlie Conner's sore foot, the result of a climb in 1929 to help survey fire damage. No trail existed at the time, and the going was especially rough.

Mount Cammerer is situated about a half mile off the AT and is a popular hike. The tower was rebuilt after the original one, built by the CCC, fell into disrepair. Cammerer is named for Arno B. Cammerer, the third director of the National Park Service. It is located in the extreme northeast section of the Great Smoky Mountains National Park.

Max Patch is one of the great southern balds—open, grassy mountain tops. There are several theories as to what created the balds. Some believe that grazing cattle, driven up to the cooler mountain tops, kept bushes and trees away. Others think that it has something to do with the soil. The Cherokee believed that a giant hornet stole children and took them to the mountain tops. Warriors pursued and the Great Spirit sent lightning and fire to kill the beast; the resulting fires swept the mountain tops clear. You, of course, are free to take your pick of these theories. Today, the balds are dwindling, and many have grown completely over. The U. S. Forest Service keeps several balds, including Max Patch, open by mowing each year.

Above: Max Patch in late fall.
Left: Max Patch under an early spring snowfall.

The white structure on Snowbird Mountain is a VOR (very-high-frequency omni-directional range) transmitting station used for aircraft navigation. Snowbird Mountain features a long ridge with the highest elevation attaining 4,263 feet.

Camp Creek Bald, on the Bald Mountains ridge, used to have a single fire tower, but is now covered by a complex of communication towers. The elevation here is 4,844 feet.

The Rhododendron Gardens on Roan Mountain are world famous. The spectacular Catawba rhododendron, with the scientific mouthful name of *Rhododendron catawbiensis,* blooms around the third week in June. Some of the oldest rocks anywhere on the AT can be found on Roan Mountain, as can the highest shelter—Roan High Knob perches at 6,285 feet.

Immediately to the northeast of Roan Mountain is a series of balds that extends for several miles. They include Round Bald, Jane Bald, Grassy Ridge, Little Hump Mountain and Hump Mountain. Together, these form the largest of all the southern balds. Hump Mountain is shown to the left, looking toward Roan Mountain, and Jane Bald is above.

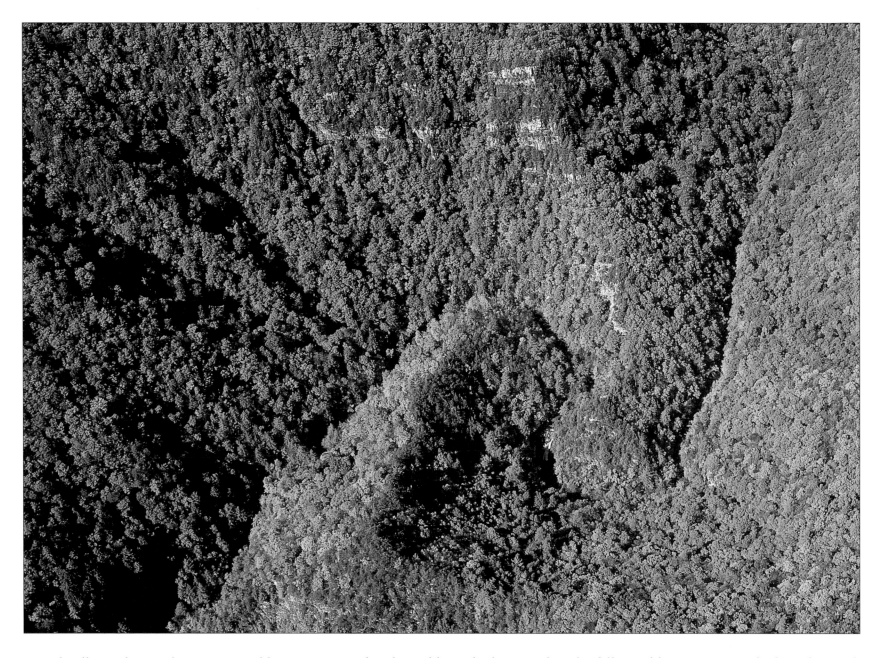

Laurel Falls, in the Pond Mountain Wilderness Area, is barely visible at the lower right. The falls tumbles approximately forty feet and, along with Laurel Fork Gorge, is a popular hiking destination.

Watauga Lake is formed by one of the largest earth and rock dams in the world. Begun in 1941, Watauga Dam was finished in 1948. Its purpose is flood control and the production of electricity for the Tennessee Valley Authority. The trail itself crosses over the top of the dam and then ascends on the right to the Iron Mountain Range.

Iron Mountain, on the right, is a fourteen mile ridge hike. Watauga Lake (left) is a major reservoir formed by Watauga Dam (preceding page). Iron Mountain is named for the extensive ore deposits that were once mined at its base. The highest elevation on the ridge is 4,150 feet. This view is to the west.

Virginia and West Virginia

The Appalachian Trail runs for 545 miles through Virginia and West Virginia, approximately one quarter of the entire length of the AT. Only fifteen or so miles of the trail run through West Virginia, and they are mostly along the Virginia-West Virginia border. The two states are covered in this chapter.

Most of the AT in this area runs through two National Forests (Jefferson in the southwest and George Washington in the middle of western Virginia). It also runs through Shenandoah National Park in the northern part of Virginia. The highest point of the trail in either state is Mount Rogers (5,729 feet) in southwestern Virginia. The lowest points of the AT are the James River crossing and Harpers Ferry, West Virginia. The trail begins in southwest Virginia and runs northeasterly through the western portion of Virginia and exits in the north at Harpers Ferry, West Virginia.

Much of the hiking through this part of the Trail is on long ridge mountains such as Garden, Brushy, Pearis, and Peters in the south and along the Blue Ridge all the way to Maryland. Places made famous in the Civil War abound. Harpers Ferry, strategically located at the confluence of the Shenandoah and Potomac rivers, was hotly contested and was the site of John Brown's unsuccessful attack on the federal arsenal located there.

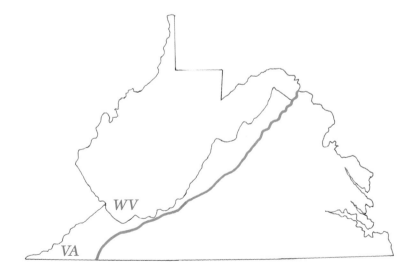

At 5,520 feet, Whitetop Mountain is the second highest peak in Virginia. The AT passes just below the peak and thus avoids the communications complex at the summit. If you look closely, you can see the trail crossing the lower part of the service road.

Preceding page: Damascus, Virginia

The highest altitude of the AT in Virginia is on Mount Rogers, at 5,729 feet. Like Whitetop, the actual trail skirts the summit about a half mile to the south. Formerly Balsam Mountain, it was renamed in 1883 for William Barton Rogers, the first state geologist of Virginia and founder of Massachusetts Institute of Technology. Mount Rogers National Recreational Area was established by Congress in 1966 and is now protected by the U.S. Forest Service, the National Park Service, the Appalachian Trail Conference, the town of Damascus, Grayson Highlands State Park and two Appalachian Trail clubs. Thomas Knob shelter is visible in the foreground.

The stone shelter on Chestnut Knob overlooks Burkes Garden, a twenty-thousand-acre oval valley that resembles a volcanic crater. The shelter was originally a fire warden's cabin.

Pearis Mountain is named for Revolutionary War soldier Captain George Pearis, one of the first settlers in this area. The long sandstone ridge (elevation about 3,400 feet) abruptly ends at the right end of the picture. There, an east facing cliff called Angels Rest overlooks the New River below. From there, the AT drops down to the river and then climbs up to Peters Mountain, another ridge hike.

Dragon's Tooth, in southwest Virginia, was formed from eroding sandstone. The sharp, craggy "fang" is a popular hiking destination.

Another popular hiking destination is McAfee Knob at the eastern end of Catawba Mountain. Over five thousand visitors a year come here. Not only are the views stunning, but the rocky projections make great settings for picture taking.

Tinker Mountain is actually a long ridge. The name may have come from Revolutionary War deserters who settled in this area. They eked out a living making pots and were known as tinkers.

Apple Orchard Mountain is not actually named for the fruit trees, but for oak trees that have been so twisted by years of winds sweeping over the four-thousand-foot summit that they now resemble apple trees. Once named Lee Mountain for General Robert E. Lee, Apple Orchard is the last tallest mountain on the AT until New Hampshire. The white dome houses radar for aviation traffic control.

A popular hike is to The Rocks, just north of Humpback Mountain, served by a side trail from the AT. The craggy greenstone ledges offer great views.

Rockfish Gap marks the southern end of Shenandoah National Park. U.S. 250 and I 64 are the two major highways that cut through the gap. It is here that the southern end of the Skyline Drive is located. This scenic roadway (right) winds a hundred or so miles along the top of the Blue Ridge to Front Royal, Virginia. The Appalachian Trail criss-crosses Skyline Drive more than thirty times.

Big Meadows campground is situated about half-way along the Skyline Drive, and is a popular stopping place for hikers. The Big Meadows complex includes the campground, a visitor center, gas station, store, lodge, laundry and showers.

Byrds Nest #2 day shelter on Hawksbill Mountain. There are five Byrds Nest shelters in Shenandoah National Park, providing refuge from mountain storms. No overnight camping has been allowed since the 1960s because of squatters taking over the shelters. Hawksbill Mountain, at 4,051 feet, is the highest in Shenandoah National Park and is located just north of the Big Meadows complex on Skyline Drive.

The scenic town of Harpers Ferry is situated on a point of land where the Shenandoah and Potomac rivers converge. It was a key objective in the Civil War. It was here that abolitionist John Brown led an ill-fated band to capture the federal arsenal in 1859. Today, Harpers Ferry is a National Historical Park. The headquarters for the Appalachian Trail Conference is located here, and the trail itself runs right through town and across the lower bridge to Maryland.

Maryland and Pennsylvania

Maryland and Pennsylvania, together with New Jersey and New York, form the mid-Atlantic States. Together, the trail runs for a little over three hundred miles through these two states. Seen from the air, the AT in this section is a series of relatively flat ridges. The highest elevation is barely above 2,000 feet in Pennsylvania.

The Appalachian Trail in Maryland is only about forty miles, almost all of it on the ridges of South Mountain. It begins on the east side of the Potomac River, across from Harpers Ferry, West Virginia, and runs northeast to the Pennsylvania border. Famous Civil War battles were fought in Maryland, notably on South Mountain and at Crampton Gap.

Like Maryland, the AT in Pennsylvania runs along flat ridges. Coal and iron played an important role in the history of this part of the country, and the remains of old foundries, smelting furnaces and charcoal pits can be seen along the trail. The last of the great ice ages descended as far south as Pennsylvania. Retreating ice deposited rocks everywhere, and the Keystone State, at least among hikers, is often referred to as Rocksylvania. Pine Grove State Park, in southern Pennsylvania, is the geographical halfway point between Georgia and Maine (although Harpers Ferry remains the psychological halfway point). Earl Shaffer, regarded as the first person to complete the AT from Georgia to Maine, was from Pennsylvania. He made his historic trip in 1948.

MARYLAND & PENNSYLVANIA

53

The crossing over the Potomac River is on a footpath along the lower railroad bridge (above). This walkway is named for Goodloe Bryon, a Maryland congressman who was instrumental in getting legislation passed in the 1970s to protect the AT. At this point, the trail is only three hundred feet above sea level. Harpers Ferry lies immediately to the left of the two bridges. On the eastern side of the bridges (right), the trail follows alongside the C&O Towpath for about three miles before climbing up South Mountain in Maryland. The towpath runs alongside the old C&O Canal, built in the mid-1800s to enable commercial vessels to navigate above the rapids here.

Preceding page: Bake Oven Knob, Pennsylvania

Gathland State Park, at Crampton Gap, Maryland, is the site of an ornate stone arch dedicated to war correspondents. George Alfred Townsend, nicknamed "Gath," was a Civil War journalist who settled on the 135-acre estate and built the memorial in 1896 as a tribute to his fellow reporters. Crampton Gap was the site of bitter Civil War fighting. The park was originally called Gapland before the Maryland legislature renamed it to honor "Gath" Townsend.

White Rocks (above, below the towers) is a Maryland cliff of whitish quartzite, hence the name. It provides views to the south. The communication towers on Lambs Knoll, above, are rumored to belong to the National Security Administration's Critical Intelligence Communications Network but who really knows? Black Rock (right) is another set of quartzite ledges. Large patches of rock tripe lichens give the rocks a dark color and are responsible for the name. There is a story that the Declaration of Independence was read here, followed by thirteen toasts—one for each of the original states—and that the revelers continued to drink "as long as a man was left with sufficient sobriety to guide his glass to his lips." The AT in this section of Maryland runs along South Mountain, just west of Camp David.

Pennsylvania's Pine Grove Furnace State Park, viewed to the west. Revolutionary and Civil War firearms were made here from iron produced by the furnace whose remains can be seen (center). The furnace, built in 1764, ran until 1895. Pine Grove is the mid-point of the AT between Georgia and Maine. The trail comes in at top center of this view, runs through the park past the furnace and exits at the bottom.

Just north of Harrisburg, the highway bridge at Clarks Ferry is the only way for the Appalachian Trail to cross the Susquehanna River. This is the longest river crossing of the entire AT. The bridge is named for Daniel Clark who operated a ferry across the river in the late eighteenth century. This is the sixth bridge to span the river since then.

Fort Snyder was built in 1756 as a lookout post for nearby (then) Fort Northkill. There was a series of these forts—one every twenty miles—to provide warning and protection to settlers from raiding Indians. A memorial plaque is all that remains of Fort Snyder. The AT comes down the hill and crosses Pennsylvania Highway 183.

The town of Port Clinton, alongside the Little Schuylkill River, marks a major transportation route through Blue Mountain for highway vehicles and railroads. The town was incorporated in 1850 and named for DeWitt Clinton, known as the founder of the Erie Canal. Port Clinton Hotel has a reputation for serving the largest cheeseburgers and the cheapest beer anywhere on the AT in Pennsylvania. This area is sometimes referred to as the buzzard capital of the northeast as these large birds use the updrafts from nearby mountains for soaring.

The Pinnacle (left) is known for providing some of the best views in Pennsylvania. Not directly on the Appalachian Trail, The Pinnacle is accessible via a short side trail. Knife Edge (above) is two hundred yards of tricky footing over the sharp, rocky and narrow ridge. Both views illustrate the infamous rocks of Pennsylvania.

Lehigh Gap cuts through Blue Mountain in eastern Pennsylvania. The Appalachian Trail descends the foreground slope and crosses the Lehigh River on the highway bridge below. The far side of the gap is the beginning of an EPA Superfund cleanup site—the result of zinc mining and smelting in nearby Palmerton. Lehigh Gap once contained a canal that was reputed to be the last in the United States to use mule power.

New Jersey and New York

New Jersey and New York complete the mid-Atlantic section of the Appalachian Trail, one of the most populated areas the trail passes through. The trail doesn't attain any great altitudes in either state, with 1,803 feet being the highest in northern New Jersey. Much of the trail here is along relatively flat ridges. Both states show evidence of the last ice age—scraped hills and mountain tops, depressions formed from melting blocks of ice and deposited rocks and boulders.

In New Jersey, the trail runs for about seventy miles, paralleling the north New Jersey and Pennsylvania border. It is mostly ridge hiking along the Kittatinny Mountain, a long ridge that extends all the way into New York State. The trail rarely exceeds 1,500 feet, with the exception of High Point State Park. Open woods, fields and pastures characterize the area.

The AT runs for about ninety miles in New York across the extreme southeast portion of the state. On most days, New York City can be seen from the higher sections of the trail. The lowest point on the whole trail is at the Trailside Zoo and Museum in Bear State Park on the western side of the Hudson River. Bear Mountain is where the familiar AT logo, with the "A" and "T" sharing a crossbar, was designed by William Welch in 1923. The very first section of the Appalachian Trail was built just south of Bear Mountain in that same year. This area was the site of much Revolutionary War activity. A giant chain was stretched across the Hudson River near Bear Mountain to keep the British from getting any further upriver. It failed, and they burned Poughkeepsie and Kingston.

63

Looking northeast at Catfish Fire Tower, perched at 1,565 feet on New Jersey's Kittatinny Mountain. Built in 1922, the fire tower is one of twenty-one that New Jersey uses for fire detection. Used only on days when there is a high probability of fire, the tower is only open to hikers when manned, and it is a popular side trip. The tower is named for nearby Catfish Pond (left), accessible from the AT via a short side trail.

Preceding page: Trail up Bear Mountain, New York

64

View looking north towards Culvers Gap over Rattlesnake Mountain. Mecca Lake can be seen to the right. The summit is at 1,492 feet, an easy number to remember (Columbus's discovery of America). This area is noted for raptor watching during spring and fall migrations as various species of hawks soar along the updrafts. Rattlesnake Mountain got its name for the reptile that may occasionally be seen here.

Culvers Gap is a major break in Kittatinny mountain. It is a wind gap, primarily formed by winds after the initial carving by a now absent river. The east end of Kittatinny Lake, a popular summer resort area, can be seen to the left. The view is looking westward.

Sunrise Pavilion on Sunset Mountain, part of the Kittatinny Mountain ridge. Built of stone by the Civilian Conservation Corps in 1937, the Pavilion provides refuge from bad weather. It is a popular day-trip destination. The elevation here is 1,653 feet.

High Point State Park (above) with its headquarters at the bottom. The park has over fourteen thousand acres and is a popular destination for day visitors and overnight hikers. There is a visitor center, several trails and a campground. The two-hundred-foot-tall monument (left) is dedicated to New Jersey war veterans. Although not actually on the Appalachian Trail, most hikers take the short detour and climb the tower for the fine views over New Jersey, New York and Pennsylvania. The monument sits at 1,803 feet, the highest point in New Jersey and the AT in that state.

An aerial view of the new boardwalk crossing Pochuck Quagmire. One of the largest building projects on the AT, it took volunteers almost seven years to complete. It spans nearly one mile over the soft and often flooded quagmire. An elevated bridge takes the hiker over Pochuck Creek, which is hidden in the trees.

Mombasha High Point, in New York, overlooks Mombasha Reservoir (upper left). The summit was scraped down to bedrock by the Wisconsin glacier, which covered this area about fifteen thousand years ago. On a clear day, a hiker can see New York City to the south.

A view from the south over Little Dam Lake. The Appalachian Trail skirts the northern shore. Once marshland, the dam was built in the nineteenth century to provide a source of water for local industry and settlers. Not far from here, Sterling Forge made the giant chain that was stretched across the Hudson River to stop the British Navy during the Revolutionary War. Today, the lake and the trail enjoy the protection of New York's Class I Wetlands Act.

Looking northeast over Bear Mountain at the bridge over the Hudson River. The stone monument was built in 1934 in memory of George W. Perkins, the first president of the Palisades Interstate Park Commission. One of the initial meetings devoted to a discussion of the Appalachian Trail was held on Bear Mountain in 1924, before the monument was built.

A view of Bear Mountain State Park's facilities (above), which include an inn, shops, playing fields, swimming pool, restaurant, picnic areas and the Trailside Zoo and Museum (immediately above the pool). The zoo contains a statue of Walt Whitman, considered by some the patron saint of hikers because of his poem "Song of the Open Road." It is also the lowest point on the entire Appalachian Trail from Georgia to Maine—only 124 feet above sea level. The Bear Mountain Bridge (left) was the longest suspension bridge in the world when opened in 1924. Nearly a half-mile in length, the span sits 135 feet above the Hudson River. It is the only way to cross the river here, and hikers must endure the traffic to get to the other side.

Crossing roads and highways can often be difficult for hikers on the AT, especially in the densely populated northeast. Getting over busy Interstate 84 is solved by the Mountain Top Road overpass. The view is looking to the north.

Connecticut and Massachusetts

The Appalachian Trail runs through these states for nearly a hundred and forty miles, fifty of them in Connecticut and ninety in Massachusetts. The mountains here are the highest since Pennsylvania and Virginia.

Of the two states, Connecticut has the lowest elevations, mostly below 1,500 feet. Even in the northern part of the state the elevation barely gets over 2,000 feet. In the south, much of the trail follows the Housatonic River, one of the longest river walks on the whole AT. The trail passes through three state forests in Connecticut: Housatonic Meadows, Kent Falls and Housatonic State, all in the western part of the state.

The AT in Massachusetts runs due north through the mountains and valleys in the extreme western part of the state. The highest point is Mount Greylock at almost 3,500 feet. What was once farmland is now mostly residential and bedroom communities for nearby cities and towns. The Appalachian Trail in Massachusetts goes right through three towns—Greylock, Cheshire and Dalton. The latter is a major producer of paper for U.S. currency.

CONNECTICUT & MASSACHUSETTS

Ten Mile Hill, with 1,000 feet of elevation, is the first climb of note in Connecticut and is just over the border from New York. The hill is named for the Ten Mile River, off to the right, which flows from its origin in New York to join the Housatonic River just below Ten Mile Hill.

Preceding page: Trail below Saint Johns Ledges

View looking down on the Ned Anderson Memorial footbridge crossing the Ten Mile River (left) immediately before its confluence with the Housatonic River. The bridge is named for a local farmer who designed and blazed the Appalachian Trail in Connecticut, finishing the task in 1933.

Indian Rocks (above) provide views to the east over the Housatonic River and Valley. The cliffs are located on the east side of the Schaghticoke Indian Reservation, just north of the confluence of Ten Mile and Housatonic Rivers. Also overlooking the Housatonic River Valley is Saint John Ledges (right), named for an eighteenth-century local landowner. The steep section on the left is a popular rock climbing area. A series of steep rock steps takes the hiker down from the ledges to the bank of the Housatonic River, which the AT then follows to the right for a little over four miles.

A view of Bear Mountain, looking north. At 2,316 feet, this is the highest elevation that the AT attains in Connecticut. The stone monument, once thirty-six feet tall, was built to mark this highest spot. Through time, the monument has crumbled and is now barely one story high.

Immediately after crossing the border into Massachusetts, the AT takes a sharp bend to the right and enters Sages Ravine. This east-west oriented gully entails almost 1,700 acres of unique wilderness. The north side of the ravine receives sunlight all day long while the south side gets almost none. This has resulted in two completely different types of plant communities. The trail runs alongside Sages Ravine Brook for nearly a mile. The ravine is named for Simeon Sage, who founded the Sage Iron Company in nearby Connecticut in the nineteenth century.

Mount Everett, at 2,600 feet, is the fourth highest mountain in Massachusetts. The fire tower was removed in 2003 but the state still has about forty others, active during the fire season. Guilder Pond can be seen in the background. The view is looking toward the north. The trail crosses over the summit next to the tower (which was removed after this picture was taken).

The Appalachian Trail goes right through the town of Dalton, in western Massachusetts (entering past the park in the lower right, then up High Street and exiting at the top, just left of center.) In 1775, Paul Revere needed Colonial currency, which he obtained from Stephen Crane's paper mill just outside Boston. Later, the company moved to Dalton and has provided all of the paper for U.S. currency since 1879. The present day Crane & Company makes paper for about eight billion bills annually.

Gore Pond (left) viewed from the southeast. This area was originally a shallow glacial lake. The AT skirts the left, or northern, side of the pond. The Cobbles (above) are just a few miles from Gore Pond. These exposed limestone and white quartz cliffs were laid bare by the last glacier to cover this area.

The highest point in Massachusetts, Mount Greylock rises to 3,491 feet above sea level. This is the first place that the AT goes over 3,000 feet since Virginia. This view to the northwest shows the summit, with its communications tower, Bascom Lodge (operated by the AMC) and the War Memorial tower. Hikers have all of the amenities here—water, food, lodging, telephone, plus superb views in all directions. On a clear day, one can see into Massachusetts, Connecticut, New York, Vermont and New Hampshire.

Vermont

The Appalachian Trail in Vermont runs for about a hundred and fifty miles. The southern section runs north from the Massachusetts border. The northern section turns to the northeast toward New Hampshire. The highest point of the AT in Vermont is Killington Peak at 4,235 feet. Killington is the second highest mountain in the state.

Much of the trail in Vermont is roughly 1,500 to 3,500 feet in elevation. The higher parts of the trail share mountain tops with some major ski areas. Recently, it has been necessary to re-locate sections of the trail as development and expansion has gotten too close.

About one-half of the trail is through the Green Mountain State Forest in the southern part of the state. The trail also goes through Coolidge State Forest, White Rocks National recreation Area and Gifford Woods State Park.

Vermont is also home of the Long Trail, whose southern end begins at the Vermont-Massachusetts border. It runs concurrent with the Appalachian Trail for about a hundred miles to Willard Gap, just north of Deer Leap, before heading north to the Canadian border. The total length of this trail is 265 miles. Begun in 1910 and finished in 1927, the Long Trail is one of the oldest hiking trails in the United States. James P. Taylor is said to have envisioned the Long Trail while hiking on Stratton Mountain, where Benton MacKaye came up with the idea for the Appalachian Trail.

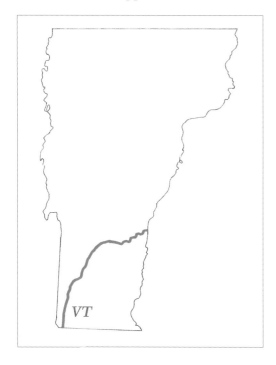

85

Less than twenty miles north of the Massachusetts-Vermont border is Harmon Hill at 2,325 feet. This view is looking to the west. The hilltop is kept open by routine burning, and it is a popular day-trip destination.

Preceding page: Willard Gap

Looking north at Glastenbury Mountain in the Green Mountain National Forest. Two-storied Goddard Shelter, at the left, is named for a former president of the AMC. Above, and slightly to the right of the shelter, is the red fire tower maintained by the U.S. Forest Service. No longer used for fire detection, the tower is open to the public, and there are plans to restore it. The summit of Glastenbury is 3,748 feet.

Stratton Mountain (above), at 3,936 feet, is one of the highest peaks in Vermont. The fire tower on the summit is open to the public and provides superb views in all directions. The ski area itself is about a thousand feet below the summit. Stratton Mountain is where Benton MacKaye envisioned the AT, when he hiked there in 1917. No camping is allowed on Stratton, but nearby Stratton Pond (left) offers shelter and camping sites. The trail skirts Stratton Pond along the southeast shore.

Prospect Rock, in the opening to the left of center, is a popular hiking destination. The Rock, jutting out from the hillside, offers fine views to the west and Manchester below. Not actually on the AT, Prospect Rock is accessible via a short side trail.

The Appalachian Trail goes over the summit of Bromley Mountain, right past the ski center buildings. The wooden observation tower can provide a good look at the surrounding countryside. The summit of Bromley is 3,260 feet, and this view is looking west.

Clarendon Gorge and Mill River looking from the south. The suspension bridge at the lower end of the gorge is dedicated to Robert Brugman, who drowned in 1973 attempting to ford the river after a flood had washed out the old bridge. Vermont Highway 103 (right) leads to Rutland. The elevation at the gorge is only 800 feet above sea level.

Looking north at the second highest mountain in Vermont, Killington Peak, at 4,235 feet. The AT skirts the actual summit—and the busy ski lift area—by-passing it to the west. Many hikers, however, make the side trip to the mountaintop for some of the finest views in Vermont.

Another mountaintop offering outstanding views is Pico Peak, at 3,957 feet. As on Killington, the trail itself does not go over the summit. The AT here was recently re-routed to the west (left of the peak) around Pico.

Deer Leap Mountain (above) and Deer Leap Rocks. The trail swings around the backside of the mountain through Willard Gap and then skirts northeast of Deer Leap Mountain. A short side trail leads down to the cliffs (right), which overlook Sherburne Pass below. This is a popular day-hike destination. The view of Deer Leap Mountain is to the north, while the view of the rocks is easterly. The Long Trail leaves the AT here and heads for Canada.

Kent Pond viewed from the south. Kent Pond is in Gifford Woods State Forest. The white building and red barn below the pond are the Mountain Meadows Lodge, a popular stopping place for hikers on the AT.

The bridge over the White River at West Hartford. The trail crosses the river here and then proceeds north alongside the road for a bit before continuing eastward. The town was called Centerville when first founded, but was later changed to Sucker City because of the fishing (or lack of it) and finally changed to West Hartford. The New Hampshire border is only seven miles to the right.

New Hampshire

In New Hampshire, the Appalachian Trail runs for about 160 miles diagonally (southwest to northeast) across the upper one-third of the state. The lower, western portion is characterized by hardwood forests, old farmlands, pastures, hills and mountains. It is the the eastern part, however, that draws hikers to its lofty ridges and peaks, much of them above tree line. The highest and most spectacular mountains in the northeast can be found in this area, especially in the Presidential Range. Much of the hiking in New Hampshire consists of radical ups and downs—peak, notch, peak, etc. Up on the Presidential Range, the hiker faces one of the most extensive mountain ridge systems on the AT.

Two-thirds of the AT in New Hampshire passes through the Green Mountain National Forest and goes through three state parks and three designated wilderness areas. There is much evidence of past glacial activity throughout New Hampshire. Notches were carved out, mountaintops were scraped down to granite bedrock and boulders litter the landscape.

When the Appalachian Trail was constructed, one of the easiest states to put the new trail in was New Hampshire, as the Dartmouth Outing Club and the Appalachian Mountain Club already had many trails in existence. It was just a matter of linking them all up. The continued influence of these two organizations is evident still, with their trail maintenance responsibilities and overseeing of huts and shelters.

Hanover, New Hampshire, on the east side of the Connecticut River. Home of Dartmouth College (center) and the Dartmouth Outing Club (DOC), the oldest such organization in the country. The Appalachian Trail comes over the bridge and to the college green before turning south (left from this view) to by-pass the rest of Hanover.

Preceding page: Beaver Brook Trail to Mount Moosilauke

Looking west at Holts Ledge. The ski trails off to the right are part of the Dartmouth Skiway. Holts Ledge has an elevation of 2,100 feet. A side trail leads to Trapper John Shelter, named for the Army surgeon in the book and movie M*A*S*H.

At 3,200 feet, Smarts Mountain offers great views of the surrounding countryside, especially from the fire tower. The old fire warden's cabin now serves as a shelter for hikers. The DOC cabin is to the left of the tower.

Four and a half miles north of Smarts Mountain is Mount Cube. The higher of its twin peaks is at 2,911 feet, with the AT passing over both of them. A good view of the White Mountains to the north can be had from here. Nearby is the popular Mount Cube Sugar House, which is said to have the best pancakes on the entire AT.

Located in the middle of the state is majestic Mount Moosilauke. An extremely popular hiking destination, Moosilauke rises to 4,802 feet in elevation. Its top was scraped bare by the last glacier in this area. A summit hotel, Prospect House, was built here in 1860. It later became the Tip Top House and was owned by the Dartmouth Outing Club as a shelter for hikers. It burned down in 1942, but the foundation remains (left). In 1927, the DOC held the first downhill ski race in America on Moosilauke.

Looking northeast at the spectacular Franconia Ridge Trail leading to Mount Lafayette. Named for the Revolutionary War general, this narrow ridge trail is a popular hike. The summit of Lafayette (right), at 5,249 feet, is the highest peak in this part of New Hampshire and above the tree line. Lafayette once had a summit hut, but all that remains is the foundation. The Appalachian Mountain Club's Greenleaf hut can be seen just beyond the summit.

Immediately east of Crawford Notch lies Webster Cliffs. The AT runs up the ridge from the right to the top of Webster Mountain. From there, it turns sharply to the right and heads for the Presidential Range. Webster Cliffs and Mountain are named for noted orator Daniel Webster. The peak is at 3,910 feet of elevation.

At 6,288 feet, Mount Washington is the second-highest Appalachian Trail peak after Clingmans Dome on the North Carolina-Tennessee border. P.T. Barnum once declared the views from here "the second greatest show on earth." Hikers need to be prepared for any kind of weather on Washington, as different weather systems frequently collide here. It can snow very early in the fall, or even during the summer months.

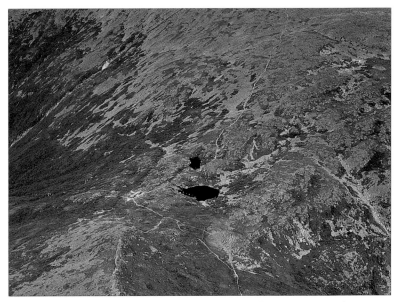

Lakes of the Clouds AMC Hut, below the summit of Mount Washington, can accommodate almost one hundred hikers.

Mount Washington's summit is also accessible by an auto road and the famous cog railway. Three steam trains can be seen creeping along on the left.

The summit of Washington has a weather observatory, museum, restaurant and various transmitting towers.

The Gulfside Trail from Washington's summit leads north to Mounts Clay, Jefferson and Adams.

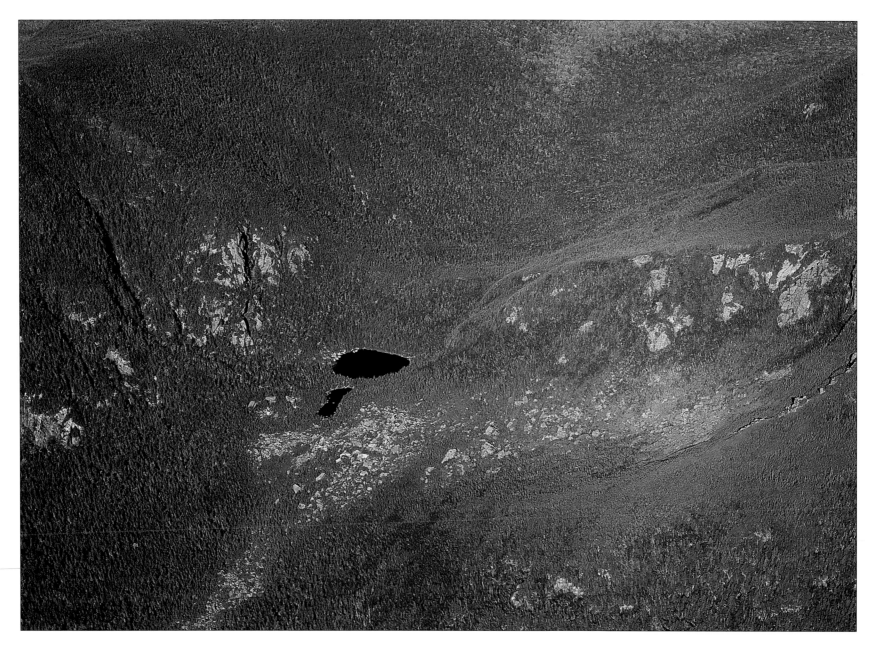

Carter Notch is a wild, rocky ravine carved by glacial activity. To the left of the smaller pond are the AMC'S two bunkhouses and a stone hut. The latter is the oldest of all AMC huts still in use (built in 1914). The trail comes down on the left, above the ponds.

View toward the north at the Androscoggin River crossing. The name is Abenaki Indian for "place where fish are aired," no doubt referring to the excellent bass fishing in this area. The AT crosses the river on the Leadmine Bridge, immediately below and parallel to the dam.

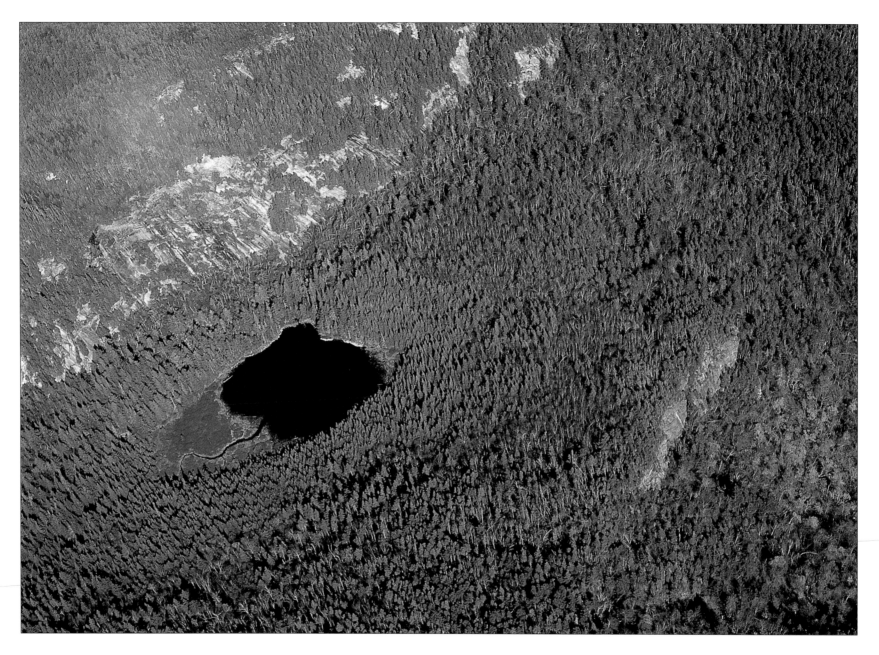

Lovely Gentian Pond, looking northwest. Austin Brook runs into the pond and exits at the lower left. The pond is named for the blue-petalled flower that grows on its wet borders. The AT runs parallel to and along the bottom of the cliffs. There is an AMC Hut campsite at the upper end of the pond.

View to the north from over the Androscoggin River toward Mount Success (above). Valley fog is slowly burning off. The summit of Mount Success (right) is at 3,565 feet. Elevated footbridges make it easier to get across the boggy summit. The wreckage of a crashed DC-3 is located just below the summit to the lower right, but is difficult to see because of the trees.

Maine

The Appalachian Trail in Maine runs for about 280 miles, in a generally northeastly direction, to Mount Katahdin in the middle of the state. The northern third of the trail is characterized by wilderness, rugged mountains, lakes, ponds, rivers and bogs. The central portion of the trail is the easiest, with only two mountains of significance to cross. The southern third is the most rugged of all, and some consider it the toughest on the entire AT, crossing seven mountains that rise above 4,000 feet and thirteen over 3,000 feet. In between there is considerable up and down hiking.

Maine was once covered by 4,000 feet of ice, with the last glacier melting about ten thousand years ago. The Maine landscape today is the result of that ice and its retreat. Most of the mountain tops have been scraped down to bedrock. Lakes, ponds, many rivers and other geological features are all glacial in origin. Katahdin's summit, however, is not the result of glacial action as the ice never extended above it. Instead, it is the result of erosion. It has been said that Katahdin is being "buried under its own ruin."

The trail in Maine is well protected by Public Reserve Lands, Baxter State Park and the National Park Service. The Maine Appalachian Trail Club maintains all of Maine's trails, except for fourteen miles of the Mahoosuc range—which are maintained by the Appalachian Mountain Club.

The first true length of the entire AT was determined by Maine native Myron Avery in 1936. It took him sixteen years, hiking the trail in sections, rolling a measuring wheel from Georgia to Maine. When the terminus sign was put up on Katahdin, he made what may be the shortest dedication speech ever recorded when he said, "Nail it up."

Maine's Goose Eye Mountain, just north of the New Hampshire border, has an elevation of 3,794 feet. The name is believed to have originated from "goose high," referring to migrating geese that fly by at eye level. This peak marks the southern end of the Mahoosuc Range.

Preceding page: trail to Spectacle Pond and the 100-Mile Wilderness

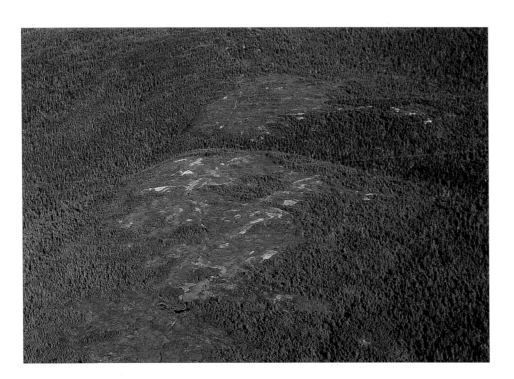

A section of the Mahoosuc Range looking south (left). There are nine peaks on the Mahoosucs over 3,500 feet. Pictured above is the famous Mahoosuc Notch, a glacier-carved, boulder-filled valley. Many hikers consider this the toughest mile on the entire AT. Here, the hiker must "climb over, crawl under, squeeze between, slide down and jump among the rocks." Many hikers are so delighted with this passage that they turn around and do it all over again.

A view of Old Spec Mountain looking north. At 4,180 feet, Old Spec is the third-highest mountain in Maine and marks the northern end of the Mahoosuc Range. The trail bypasses the summit by going around to the northwest. The old fire tower is no longer used for fire detection and has been converted to an observation tower open to the public.

Baldpate Mountain looking west (left). Baldpate has two peaks, West Peak, at 3,662 feet and East Peak, at 3,812 feet. The latter, more open summit, offers superb views. Baldpate is a very popular day hike. (Above) View to the north over East Peak.

Two seasonal views of Saddleback Mountain, both looking east. A popular ski center as well as hike, Saddleback has 4,120 feet of elevation. The name is said to have originated because when seen from afar, the mountain resembles a saddle.

Looking west over Flagstaff Lake at the Bigelow Range (above). Many consider Bigelow the most outstanding range in Maine. The highest summit is West Peak at 4,145 feet. Avery Peak (left) is named for Myron H. Avery, who first measured the entire length of the AT. He was the Chairman of the ATC from 1933 to 1952. The stone fire tower is not open to the public.

The most dangerous river crossing on the whole AT is Maine's Kennebec River at Caratunk. A large dam, twenty miles upriver, releases water at unscheduled and unannounced intervals. The onrush would overwhelm anyone attempting to ford the river, so Maine's Appalachian Trail Club runs a free canoe ferry service across the river from late May into early October. In this view, the canoe is beached on the west bank of the river.

The granite summit of Moxie Bald Mountain, looking to the west. Moxie Bald is located on the west side of Bald Mountain Pond and rises to 2,629 feet above sea level. The open summit provides excellent views. The soft drink Moxie originated in Maine, hence the name.

View from Monson looking toward Mount Katahdin across the 100-Mile Wilderness. There is no place where hikers can stop for supplies in the next hundred miles, so they must stock up in Monson (right). The town has variety and general stores, lodging and food. The AT does not go through Monson, but passes a few miles to the north.

Barren Ledges looking to the northeast. The summit of Barren Mountain, at 2,270 feet, lies just to the right of the picture. Barren Mountain was once known as Slate Mountain.

The "Grand Canyon of Maine," Gulf Hagas is not directly on the AT, but the trail passes just to the east, and most hikers take the side trip. The 3-mile-long box canyon was carved by the West Branch of the Pleasant River, which still runs through it. A rim trail provides views down on the spectacular gorge. Gulf Hagas is on the National Natural Scenic Register.

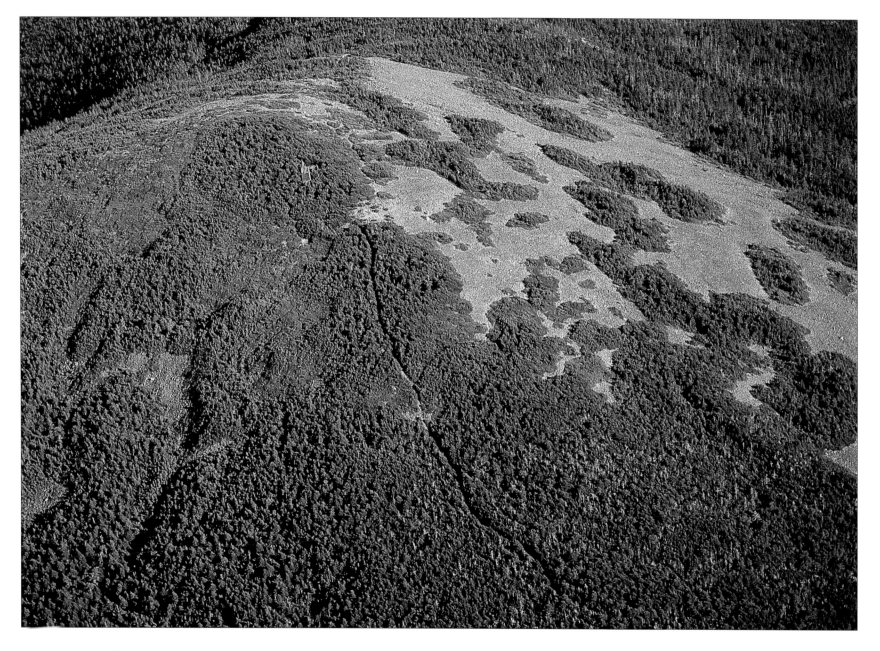

The summit of White Cap Mountain, at 3,654 feet, is the highest point in this area and offers great views to the north, especially of Katahdin. The name comes from the slow snow melt, making the mountaintop white until late spring. The remains of an old fire tower can be seen near the summit.

Aptly named Crescent Pond, looking to the north. The AT follows the northern (upper) shoreline and then comes down the east side before heading off to the right. Crescent Pond is a true glacial tarn (mountain lake).

View to the northeast of the Hunt Trail leading to the summit of Katahdin. For thru-hikers, the Hunt Trail marks the end of their long journey. At 5,267 feet in elevation, Katahdin falls short of being a mile high, but a 13-foot stone cairn on the summit makes up the difference. Katahdin comes from the Abenaki Indian word *Kette-Adene,* meaning "highest land" or "greatest mountain." The centerpiece of Baxter State Park, Katahdin rises all by itself from the surrounding countryside, rather than being part of a mountain range.

The upper end of the Hunt Trail to the summit of Katahdin. The boulder-strewn mountain top is the result of freezing and thawing cycles after the last ice age melted away.

Katahdin's summit overlooks a huge glacial cirque.

The Knife Edge Trail, east of the summit. This trail is not part of the AT, but many hikers cannot resist it.

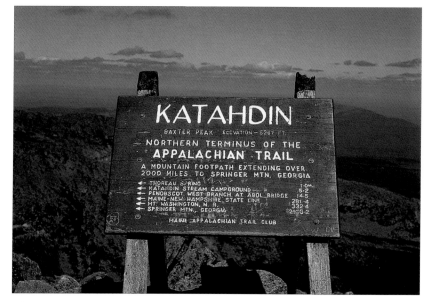

The sign marking the northern termins of the AT.

Conclusion

In 1995, while living in Connecticut, I had the opportunity to buy a 1947 Piper Cub PA-12 Super Cruiser at a price that I could afford. The airplane needed a complete rebuild and new cover over its tube frame—a three-year project. Near the end, a good friend stopped by for dinner. He was interested in the airplane restoration but really wanted to talk about his recent hiking on the Appalachian Trail. It was easy to catch his enthusiasm, and I soon obtained and read Bill Bryson's book *A Walk in the Woods.* I became more interested in the trail and, with a local pilot in his airplane, flew to western Connecticut, where the nearest part of the AT was located. I was hooked the moment I saw the footbridge crossing the Ten Mile River. Here was something I could do with the airplane—show people what the trail looked like from the air. My plan to sell the Super Cruiser for a profit was quickly replaced with the idea for an aerial AT book.

Ten Mile River Crossing

With the airplane completed and tested, I needed some tailwheel instruction (I had only flown nose wheel aircraft). Finishing that, I immediately flew the Super Cruiser to Florida's Annual Sun 'n Fun air show. On the way down and back I thought of the AT and how to approach the task of locating parts of the trail from the air and photographing them.

Shortly after that trip, we moved from Connecticut to Maine, and I paid a visit to DeLorme, the great map-making company in Yarmouth. They had just begun putting latitude and longitude on their Atlases and Gazetteers. The problem of how to get the positions of AT sections that I wanted was solved.

The following year, I flew to Sun 'n Fun via the Appalachian Mountains, taking pictures on the way down and back. The results were encouraging, and I began making subsequent flights in earnest. When I couldn't get south because of weather or other problems, I drove down and prevailed upon local pilots to fly me around. From beginning to end, the project took almost five years.

PA-12 Super Cruiser
(photo by Rod Bradley)

The Super Cruiser was difficult to photograph from. I had to awkwardly lean back and stick the camera out a small window in the door. I clearly needed a different airplane if I was going to do the job right. I knew the aircraft I wanted, and in November of 2002, I located a 1959 Piper Super Cub in Oklahoma. Its

PA-18 Super Cub
(photo by Helen Wander)

horizontally hinged window, when up, opens the whole side of the airplane—a perfect airborne camera platform. I flew the Super Cub back via the Appalachian Trail and kept my camera busy the whole trip.

My routine was to read everything I could get my hands on about the AT during the winter months and fly during the rest of the year. I determined the latitude and longitude of what I wanted to photograph and entered them into a small hand held GPS (Global Positioning System) unit. When flying, I called up the position I wanted, and the GPS steered me to it. I then made sure that I had the right place, figured out how to best photograph the site—light angle, altitude, angle to the site and so on. Then I slowed the airplane down, opened the window and took the pictures, holding the Cub steady with my knees on the stick. It usually took three circuits, sometimes more. It bothered me when hikers were present, and I did what I could to mitigate disturbing them. I would fly to a higher altitude, throttle back and glide past the mountain, taking pictures as I went. Most hikers appeared friendly and tolerated my presence for a few minutes. A Cub with a 90-horse engine doesn't make much noise anyway, but I apologize to anyone I may have offended.

My photographic equipment consisted of an old Nikon F2 camera with a 55mm macro lens. I prefer that lens for aerial work as it produces very sharp images and is a flat field lens—the pictures are just as sharp at the edges as in the center. My favorite film was Fujichrome Velvia RVP 50, an extremely fine-grained slide film, but slow in speed. I found that a shutter speed of $^1/_{250}$ second was enough to obtain clear blur-free photographs, especially on days of calm winds—a rarity in the mountains.

The views from a small airplane are unique, refreshing and often thrilling. I'm not sure of my next project, but I hope it will be from the Cub, now undergoing its restoration.